I0115794

BROOKFIELD THE JUNGLE

THE LIFE OF ANDREW WADSWORTH / THE PASSING OF ANTONIO YOUNG

EAST OAKLAND TIMES, LLC

EAST
OAKLAND

Copyright © 2019 by EAST OAKLAND TIMES, LLC

All rights reserved.

No part of this book may be reproduced in any form or by any electronic or mechanical means, including information storage and retrieval systems, without written permission from the author, except for the use of brief quotations in a book review.

To conquer oneself is a greater victory than to conquer thousands in a battle.

— THE 14TH DALAI LAMA, TENZIN GYATSO

MY CRIME SERIES - BOOK SEVEN - BROOKFIELD THE JUNGLE

Welcome to San Quentin State Prison! Come and meet your new "celly." His name is Andrew Wadsworth and he has a story to tell about the pull of the streets and the path of redemption.

The books of the My Crime series are neither meant to justify nor condemn the inmates on whom they are written. Rather, the books of the My Crime series propose to candidly communicate the upbringing, life experience, and motivations of the incarcerated.

The My Crime series puts you as the judge. Your judgment will not simply be about the individual on whom a book is written, but your judgment will weigh the life circumstances that shaped his or her criminal disposition. The My Crime series takes the unknown inmate and presents his or her life for public evaluation.

Each book in the My Crime series is written on an inmate, by an inmate. Each book will progress from the subject's childhood up through the commitment offense that brought about the subject's current felony incarceration. Each book, therefore, will offer a window into the subject's criminality as dictated to and written by a fellow inmate.

The My Crime series books are intended to fit into the present day dialog on crime and punishment. As citizens of California's democracy within the United States, the understanding we each have of right and wrong is the most essential knowledge we can use in taking political positions. Ideally, the justice issued by state, county, city, and, potentially, regional lawmakers, as interpreted by the courts, is a justice that agrees with citizens. If citizens agree with the justice being issued by an elected government, citizens will tend to promote that justice as truth for the times.

The My Crime series intends to bring Californias together in an understanding of the life experience of California felons. Through the My Crime series, you gain the opportunity to sit and listen to the unknown felon and learn, as if you were on the bottom bunk, about your neighbor and what brought him or her to getting locked up.

Thank you for purchasing the seventh book in the My Crime series.

PLEASE REVIEW BROOKFIELD - THE JUNGLE ON AMAZON!

I welcome you to visit the webpage dedicated to this series to find more crime biographies and audio interviews.

WWW.CRIMEBIOS.COM

Finally, read the last page of this book for a broad understanding of the philosophy of the producer of the My Crime series, the East Oakland Times, LLC.

Tio MacDonald
Founder & Chief Editor

ANDREW WADSWORTH

My name is Andrew Wadsworth Jr. I'm currently serving a term of 50 years to life for the crime of first-degree murder. My crime occurred in the streets of Brookfield. I'm a native from East Oakland California. I was raised by two loving parents by the names of Andrew Wadsworth Sr. And Carolyn Denise Wadsworth. My inception into this world occurred November 26th, 1984, at Highland Hospital in Oakland, CA.

The "game," the hustling, the selling, the banging, and dealing are referred to as the game. But truthfully it's not a game at all. The game can be played where you can really lose your life. You can lose your life anywhere at any God-given time. But in this game, your chances for survival are higher when that's all you know. When people grow up in an environment where drugs are penetrating the heart of the neighborhood and where parents have fallen victim to the powerful disease of addiction. Where a large percentage of families are traumatized by the damaging circumstance of being a fatherless household. This can be due to incarceration or other unfortunate events. It's not hard to see how the game seems to be the only option. One that's lucrative enough and more obtainable than the average 9-5 paying job. High paying jobs don't seem achievable. You will eventually become a product of the game. This is how it happened to me.

✖ ✖ ✖

As a baby, I was very handsome. I was born with long curly hair. My hair was the topic of most of my dad's conversations with friends. The only downside was that I cried a lot and many people would tell my parents, "Don't bring that boy over here. He cries too much." I was told my grandma uttered this many times as she couldn't stand my crying. I was what was called a "little big head boy." A feature that I'm still blessed with. As I was in my early years of life, my main man, my dad, would always make sure I was bathed and had on clean clothes. He would always make sure I was in tow when he would go back and forth to my granny's house. We would just sit around and watch T.V. shows or movies when he wasn't high on crack.

My mother and father were married for 38 years. Inside my household, there was daily drug use for as long as I could remember. My parents would use drugs so much that they walked around looking like human zombies. Their movements were fast and unorthodox all hours of the day and night. This left me with many sleepless nights wondering about the things that could get my parents hurt. They would try and hide their drug use from me at times by giving me money to go to the arcade for the day. They would smoke crack all day while I was gone. I would take the money willingly and sit at the arcade playing games until midnight when the store would close.

When this occurred, I would then roam around the streets of Oakland by myself breaking windows on cars that were parked on the streets. Maybe this was my way of rebelling what was going on at home. I would then quickly look in the vehicles and steal whatever valuables that were in them. I also frequented grocery stores and took little snacks to keep my belly full during this time. When I was extremely bored, I would play doorbell ditch. A game in which I would ring someone's doorbell and run away before anyone came to answer it. Most of the time I got away clean, but a few times the police would pull me over and ask if I was "Andrew." They would then tell me that my parents were looking for me. I was around 12 years old at this time. I couldn't believe it, maybe my parents had thought that I had run away from home. Truthfully it wasn't home that I was running away from but their addiction to drugs.

My dad was never into any gangs and was deemed a square (ordinary citizen) by most. The only odd thing I could say about him was his build. He was so thin I would joke with him saying he looked like Pee Wee Herman. He was aggressive and wild. He grew up attending Catholic schools and had a full military career with an honorable discharge. The only dissolution to their marriage was his death by murder at 56 years of age.

My dad became addicted to crack cocaine late in life. To support his habit he committed white collar crimes in the areas we resided. His last employment was at a bank as a bank teller where he used to steal money from the cash tills. After my dad retired, we lived off of his disability check that totaled around $4,000 a month. This allowed for a higher quality of life to be present for my family.

My mother was educated and a very loving person. She spent a lot of time making home cooked meals and worked various jobs over her lifetime. My mother's ambition motivated her to seek better positions, so she left many jobs. Eventually, my parents lived solely off of my dad's disability checks.

My mom and dad were full of love towards each other; yet if you listened to the way they spoke to each other, you would think otherwise. They used profanity so much you'd assume it was acceptable language. They meant no harm to each other it was just the way they talked. My dad was loving and dedicated to my mother despite how they showed a lack of affection in public. He was very generous and protective of his family. As a result, my mother was very dependent upon him for her survival. He depended on her for emotional support. They were truly inseparable even when in our home together. He would yell her name all day long for no reason. Their only hindrance was their addiction to crack cocaine.

LIVING WITH MY PARENTS

I was blessed and very fortunate to have both parents living at home with me. That was uncommon in most of my friends' houses. However, living with my parents was always unstable. It was mostly due to their drug addiction. Though my mom was sweet and cool, calm, and collected, there was an emptiness in our home. My dad's set income from the Veterans Assistance (V.A.) compensation that he coupled with his Social Security check income allowed us for some time to live a very fortunate lifestyle. We had a brief stay traveling abroad in Alaska and Reno, Nevada. Then we had to move back to Cali because of disturbance issues as the cops were frequently called to our home.

We traveled around the Bay area for a while. We lived in various cities such as Fremont, Hayward, San Leandro, and San Lorenzo, California. Our usual stay in these different cities was brief and no longer than a year. We stayed in a top-grade apartment complex that had a swimming pool inside of it. The police were called on many occasions based on how often and frequent my parents would fight. If the police weren't the reason for bouncing around cities, it would be for safety concerns because of something underhanded that my father had done. He always had one con or another brewing up. The downside about our continuing to move around was I seemed to find myself in a different school every six months. We finally settled down in Oakland, California.

My grandmom on my mom's side was named Roberta Johnson. Unfortunately, she passed away before I was born. Her passing left my mom's dad, who was named Arthur Johnson, alone; everyone called him "Poppa." I think the passing of my grandmom on my mom's side was the catapult to my mom experimenting with crack. I don't know whether it was my mother or father that created their drug use. All I know is they initially used cocaine recreationally.

✖ ✖ ✖

A little later in life, I would be out roaming the streets with an older friend named "Sky" (Rest in Peace.) Sky would school me about selling crack cocaine and weed. See, running the streets would help me pull things together mentally. There was one particular time I was hanging out with Sky and we were going to Kentucky Fried Chicken (KFC.) Sky asked me to hold his weed and, of course, I agreed as I wanted to be accepted by my friend. Someone came up to us as we were walking and asked for a bag of weed. Sky looked over at me and nodded. I handed over the bag of marijuana and collected the money. It was my first drug deal. I smiled to myself as I quickly pocketed the money. I felt as if I had graduated into a life of wealth.

When you want to sell drugs, it's not really hard. All you got to do is have a good product. Once people know you got good drugs for sale, they'll actually come looking for you. The dilemma was keeping my money and also my new job a secret from my parents. Sky said he would give me about 10 rocks to start with.

Each crack rock was worth around $10. If I sold the crack at the end of the day, he would always make sure I had money in my pocket. This gave me money to buy candy and food.

After the learning scenario with Sky, I paid attention to people on the streets like I was studying for an exam at school. Daily I watched the older guys that were known on the streets by terms like "Original Gangsters" (O.G.'s) or "Baby Gangsters" (B.G.'s) I watched them closely, observing how they did transactions and behaved as potential customers pulled or walked up. I watched them migrate to other areas of Oakland as customers on the "Flatlands" slowed up during certain times of the month.

They had shifts on each block in the Flatlands. There could be a day in which you only made pocket change selling drugs or days when you earned over $1,000. The only thing that affected the amount of money made was the police presence. One officer in particular named T. Jones kept filing federal indictments against specific dealers in the Flatlands. These indictments would be an injunction ruled on by federal judges precluding people from standing on particular street corners. This made drugs addicts travel to the other side of the tracks to shop for their product.

Now that I knew what crack was and how it was sold, home became a harder place to live. I found it hard at times to look my parents in the eye when they came home. It was not that I was ashamed of them at this time, but I was angry because they were hiding what they did from me.

✖ ✖ ✖

L iving with my parents had more downs than ups. I did, however, like the cash that I would get while staying with them. My dad would give me $100 as soon as he broke his check. He told me I could spend it however I wanted. I would mostly spend the money on candy and clothes. The sad part was my dad would get his veteran and social security checks on the 1st of each month and, within a few days, my parents would spend all the money on drugs. Also, all the new clothes that I bought or they bought for me could be sold by my parents to get high. Many of our neighbors had a boy my age or my size in their homes, so for my dad selling my clothes was easy. I adapted by wearing layers of clothes. Even if I had to put on multiple outfits in one day, I did. I, however, loved the fact that it was just my parents and me most of the time at home. Despite our dysfunctional home, I was blessed to have both parents at the house. Again, this was a rare situation in the Oakland streets of Brookfield.

Living at home with my parents and watching them abuse cocaine eventually took a toll on my mind. Seeing their struggle with addiction and watching rap videos on T.V. made me think that there had to be a better way. The videos would alter my perception of how easy it was to have everything in life. Rap videos were all I really had to maintain my sanity. I really didn't have many friends during these years. My solitude was mostly because I was afraid to bring someone home, so I kept everything bottled up and was a loner. The only youngsters I could really depend on were my cousins, Quameeka and Anthony. We shared a passion for watching movies together like "Menace to Society" and "Boys in the Hood," which we considered gangster movies. It gave all of us something to emulate. Rap music gave us a vocabulary to mimic. This made our young minds feel grown.

As the months passed into years, I learned to look outside the home for influence. It was the older kids standing on the street corner that piqued my interest. They had money, cars, and nice clothes, but never went to school. All they did was sell drugs on corner blocks.

The initial thoughts that I had about selling drugs were the fear of being robbed or killed as a result. However, the code I adapted was if I sold drugs I could make it. This resulted in all neighborhood kids feeding off of each other's energy and success. This was our code for being drug dealers.

I don't blame my parents for my poor decisions, but I do think their addiction to crack significantly influenced my life. I believe their trauma influenced my poor decision making. My rationale was that crime was a necessary fact of life. I was always unsure about what could occur to me because of what my parents did. I was also concerned about the way they looked while on a drug binge. It was as if they didn't care about their appearance or even showered. Then my fear turned into shame. I felt ashamed for them and how they allowed crack to be their world. I always wanted to be their world. It hurt me to have any friends come around while they were on a drug binge. I would see how my friends would look at them and shake their heads at me. This shame turned into anger. I was angry at my parents for allowing themselves to want the drugs more than they did me. This was at least the way I felt. The ironic part was to them drug addiction became normal. I guess it was an acceptance of their addiction as a lifestyle.

I couldn't deal with seeing them high every day. Seeing all the furniture in our home being sold so they get high was the breaking point for me. My dad would sell my personal clothes, which angered me tremendously, so staying at home was out of the question. I couldn't keep anything of value there.

I can remember at one point I even sold crack cocaine to my dad. This admittance is nothing that I'm proud of. And in no way a highlight of my childhood. The fact that I would get them high is something I look back on with regret. I never wanted to get them high. But since I was hustling, I might as well get money. The fact was my parents were getting high daily. I had the product, so why let the next man get the money. In the back of my head, I think I justified my action as a way of getting back all of the money my dad stole from me over the years. I reasoned mentally that as long as I wasn't selling it to my dad at the full street price, then I really wasn't selling it to him. All I was doing was making my money back with each transaction. My parents' addiction to cocaine came to a head and made me move in with my grandparents.

MY GRANDPARENTS & LIVING
WITH THEM

My grandmother's name is Esther. She worked as a janitor at the Oakland Airport. She worked at the job for 40 years. My grandfather is named Henry. He was a World War II veteran who also served briefly in Vietnam before retiring. At this time he worked part-time as a golf course manager. They are the legacy behind the Wadsworth family. It was their union that made all of us possible.

My grandparents are my rock. They always have been and showed all of us the life we could have. Our every basic need was provided for in their home. They gave us all that we could ever want. We went on trips to the Virgin Islands and New Orleans, Louisiana, to name a couple hot spots. They are the most loving and caring people I have ever met in my life.

Living with my grandparents was very different from staying at home with my parents. There could be no comparison of living with my grandparents versus my mom and dad. In my grandparents' home, there were morals and values to abide by. It was a house of love. While living with my mom and dad was a house and a life filled with the immoral.

At first, there were brief stays with my grandparents. I stayed there with my two cousins, named Meeko, who was a year older than me, and Anthony, who was two years older than me. We all lived in my grandparents five-bedroom home. My grandparents had their own room, of course. Anthony and I shared a room in the den, which normally would have been a cozy place to gather but was converted into a bedroom by my grandparents for us to sleep in. Meeko slept in her own room. Their home was located in Brookfield Village. My new abode was in East Oakland, a little off of 98th Avenue. We stayed on Clara St. Our granny was old fashioned and required us to go to church every Sunday. We all wore our "Sunday best" to church, which usually was a suit and tie for the boys and a long flowing dress for Meeko. Their home was a safe and clean environment for us to thrive in, a night and day comparison to living with my parents. Here no drug addiction was tolerated.

Both of my grandparents had a way of preparing a meal. They both could cook very well and made sure we all had a hot meal to eat every night. They also made sure we had new school clothes to wear as each school semester started. Their only requirement was that we went to school and studied hard.

At the beginning of my 9th year of life, I had a run-in with the law. It was due to me breaking into a daycare center located in an apartment complex. There was no real reason for me to break into this place. I just probably wanted to play with the toys. I was buzzed and wasn't thinking right. I had been sneaking drinks of liquor that day, which had me dizzy. Older kids had a bottle. I thought if I only had a little bit of it, Granny wouldn't notice. Someone must have seen me go into the place for the next thing I knew, flashlights were shining in my face. It was the police and the thought of them made me a little nervous. As one grabbed me by the arm, I threw up and sprayed alcohol all over his pants legs. Once placed into the squad car, I threw up again. I was released later that day into my grandparents' custody. My granny was more concerned with me being drunk than me being caught in the daycare center. I couldn't explain it and just fell asleep.

From as early as I could remember, those around me thought that I was mentally underdeveloped, yet I was still curious about everything around me. This curiosity went on until I was around 10 years of age. Around that time, I began to prove myself. Many people around me would dare me to do something as they knew I would do it. It was as if I didn't think that any action, whether dangerous or not, had any consequences. I just wanted acceptance, so doing the crazy things requested of me made me feel a part of something bigger than myself.

I started seriously selling drugs around the age of 12 or 13. I had been around drugs since I was an infant (as far back as I could remember.) At home, I hung around the addicts as they got high and then "tweaked" (a term used for people's reaction to crack cocaine) like zombies. The smell of burning crack became common to me. Although I did hate direct contact smoke as it made me feel strange when I breathed it in. Still, if rock cocaine was just in the air, I was used to the smell. As I got older, I would tell users, "It's cool to do what you do. Just blow the smoke out the window." Basically, away from me. Sometimes I would even let them smoke crack in my "hooptie," (a barely running car) but directed them to blow the smoke out the window. It didn't bother me because my parents raised me while they smoked crack daily.

My next run-in with the law was due to possession of crack cocaine. It was only one rock. What occurred was I was pulled over one day by the Oakland Police Department (OPD), which I had seen driving down the road. I was still in my early teens. I had my bag of rocks cheeked (held between my butt cheeks), so I felt safe. As they approached the usual questions ensued and, of course, I was patted down for weapons. Next to the squad card, as one of the police patted me down, the bag must have come open because one rock rolled down my leg and there was nothing I could do. The officer saw the rock on the ground and arrested me. He took me down to the police station to be booked.

Sitting in the police station intake tank had me very nervous. I still had about 8 rocks cheeked. I imagined that they wanted to strip search me eventually to see if I had any more drugs concealed on my person. I was still handcuffed behind my back at this time. I had enough play in the handcuffs to reach between my butt cheeks and grab the bag of crack. It was my once in a lifetime chance. There was a trash can just within pitching distance. As the officer that was sitting at the intake desk looked away, I pitched the bag from a sideways angle towards the large trash can that was only a few feet away. I had one shot and basically, this would be the shot of my short life. With all of my will, the rocks flew from my hand and successfully fell into the trash. I could have sworn the bag paused on the rim of the can as if it wanted to drop on the floor but slowly slide its way into the trash. I was fortunate to be able to do this before a full search was performed. It was my first real teenage offense and since I was a juvenile, they elected to book and release me. Sort of lucky and crazy how everything occurred.

My grandparents loved all of us but seemed to be more concerned with the basics of putting a roof over our heads than concerned with what was going on with us mentally. They felt as long as the kept food in our bellies that God would carry us the rest of the way.

The next time I had a run-in with the law was when I was at one of the local corner drug spots. I usually would keep my marijuana pinned to my shirt. This made it very accessible when I needed to retrieve a bag to sell. I also had about 19 crack rocks in my back pocket. My mind was in a different place as I sat shooting dice with others from the block. Out of nowhere, two unmarked police cars pulled up. The vice squad and marshals quickly exited, before anyone could try to flee the scene, immediately drawing their guns, and demanding everyone line up side by side. They took their time, methodically moving down the line searching each person. After about 20 minutes, they were making their way closer to me. I was shaking like a leaf in the wind. I had enough drugs on me to send away for a while. As the officer approached me and began his search, he was a little tired. At first, he patted me down lightly. This gave me the impression that it was not going to be an extensive search of my person. Well, this was my thought pattern until he opened one of the panels to my coat. Initially, he closed it quickly, but then, as he was closing the panel, he noticed something. He re-opened my jacket and as clear as day there was the weed pinned to my shirt. He immediately put me in handcuffs and walked me to the squad car. Before he placed me in the car, he walked away momentarily to talk to another officer. As he walked away, I immediately reached into my back pocket and grabbed the bag of crack rocks. I couldn't pitch them anywhere as I was pressed against the side of the car. Any quick movement would draw unwanted attention. All I could do was drop the sack of rocks on the ground. They landed on the front tip of my shoe. I tried with all my might to kick the bag of small rocks under the unmarked car. Finally, they left my foot and landed just under the car. I felt a false sense of relief for as the cop was returning to place me in the car a gust of wind blew. I assume by the bag being so small and light it blew the bag of rocks back into plain view from under the car. The bag was now highly visible at my feet. My heart dropped as the officer bent down and picked up the bag of crack. There was nothing I could do but smile as he placed me into the back of the car. I was then transported to the local substation to be booked and processed into the juvenile part of the county jail.

If that wasn't enough when I was released into my parents' custody on informal probation, I had another run-in with the law a few days later. It was the 4th of July. I went into a local convenience store to buy some snacks to satisfy the munchies. It was a day of celebrating and I had smoked a marijuana blunt earlier. I grabbed a bag of chips on which I put chili and nacho cheese on top. I then sprinkled a little jalapeno and went to the beverage area and grabbed a soda. I snacked on my hand-made chili cheese nachos on my way to the counter. When I finally made it to the checkout stand, the attendant wanted to charge me an extra dollar for the stuff I put on my chips. I had never been charged before and wasn't going to pay now. The attendant began arguing and shouting at me. It turned into a heated argument. He tried to shove me and then grabbed at my shirt. In the process, he grabbed my gold necklace chain. I immediately punched the guy so he would let me go. It turned into a full fight. In the process, someone must have called the police. As I heard the sirens approaching, I ran fleeing the store and went home. Making it home, I felt safe. I stayed inside for about 30 minutes and then walked back outside to see what was going on for the holiday. I knew everyone was barbecuing and would pop fireworks. As soon as I walked out the front door, a squad car stopped in front of my house. As the cop exited the vehicle, the first thing he shouted was, "Where is the gun at?" My reply was, "What?" He didn't ask again, as another squad car pulled up to a screeching halt.

Oakland Police Department wasn't known for following the law; they entered the home without a search warrant and searched the house for a gun and placed me in handcuffs, taking me to the local jail. I was on probation at the time, so I assume that is how he legally did so. I was booked on assault charges. I spent a couple of months walking around the juvenile jail pending trial. My lawyer quickly settled on a plea disposition. The judge in the case elected to place me on an electronic ankle monitor. He told my lawyer it was a deterrent for me committing more crimes. This was an unconditional part of the plea that I had to accept. The ankle monitor sort of made me feel like a caged animal, but it was better than walking around the jail.

When released this time, my granny made me stay at her house. My granny was too strict and staying in the house all day just wasn't an option. She wouldn't let me do anything. All I could hear was her ranting about me staying out of trouble and not going back to jail. One day as I left the house to go to the store, I launched my plan. I would place what my next move was on the flip of the coin: heads, I would cut the ankle bracelet off and tails I would leave it on. The coin landed on tails which was against my plans, so I flipped the coin again. This time it landed on heads and I smiled. I crept back into the house to grab some clothes and pulled out a pocket knife to cut off the bracelet. As I placed the knife on the bracelet, I noticed a gold wire hung between the plastic. It was a trip wire and when I cut it knew I only had minutes to make it out of the house. It was said and done. The next day, I failed to report to my probation officer as scheduled, having elected to cut the ankle monitor off. I knew the cops would be looking for me, but I needed to have a little fun. I was eventually arrested and spent a few weeks in juvenile hall before I was released on formal probation.

BROOKFIELD

Brookfield is an area located around the corner from the Oakland Coliseum. The sports venue brought a lot of traffic to our area at all times of the year. There was also a Bay Area Rapid Transit (BART) station on Hegenberger Road. There was also a lot of hotels in this area. In Brookfield, you had a well-known recreational center that many teens frequented. It was almost as popular as a mall as far as a hangout spot goes. For many people, the rec center was a place to check in when coming to Brookfield, but for those of us that lived here, it was like headquarters.

Brookfield is a neighborhood filled with houses and has a few apartments in it, but mostly houses. Basically, for those of us living there, it was a decent residential area. I don't think anyone there considered Brookfield a dangerous environment. It just had a lot of drug dealing going on. This usually involved a cat and mouse game with the local police department. The police job was to catch you and yours was to keep getting away. The cops would pop up out of nowhere and as long as you had nothing illegal on you, you're good. There weren't many people from other areas in our neighborhood, so the police sort of knew people by name and face. Everyone seemed to know everybody.

I was enjoying my freedom. My birthday rolled around. I was now 16 years old and felt like I was grown. I loved walking the streets of Brookfield. It was where I felt most comfortable.

I had become a gang member at this time. I knew everyone and it seemed like everyone knew my family or me. 98th Avenue in Brookfield is the biggest turf (area of gang members) in East Oakland. I was part of a gang called Brookfield Jungle Boys (BJB). BJB is was what people called us. The area wasn't a jungle, but many had adapted to the saying that "It's a jungle out there," and used the phrase for where we lived.

The Jungle had many city blocks within its area such as the Flat-lands and Storefront, which is a strip of 98th Ave. Darien and Eldridge (D.E.), Dagvile, Columbian Garden's (C.G), Quad Village (Q.V.), and Douglas: all of these blocks are in Brookfield. The blocks had many different names, but we called the entire area Brookfield. The only time any particular street name or area came into discussion was when we yelled out to each other. That's how we used to brag about particular blocks.

There was also a park in my neighborhood which had plenty of room to run around in. My family always threw picnics at this park. People in the neighborhood would throw picnics there also. The park was located in the Flatlands, so many of us called it "Flatland Park." The annual picnic was called the "Flatland Picnic." The picnic gathering would grow so large it was referred to as a summer jam concert. There were many beautiful women. Some were from the area and others had traveled miles for the experience. You had a few people that were either in the drug trade or just pimped women. We called the people that would always be at the Flatland Picnic, "legends."

These legends made Brookfield famous in the eyes of residents that lived there and those from neighboring areas. What really brought these people status to be legendary was that they were talked about in many rap songs. The major record label that produced these artists was called "Notorious Pimps, Playas, and Hustlers," which mostly produced compilation compact disks. The owner of the company was a man named Vee. He looked just like Dennis Rodman. His first collaboration CD sold 200,000 copies locally in Oakland alone. You may not consider 200 K a significant number, but for an independent label, that's huge. He had a lot of Oakland rappers included in this compilation, artists like - The Delinquents, Dru Down, Rappin Ron, Ant Diddley Dog, and 3x Krazy. There were many more unknown artists, but the listed were the hot selling points. Most of these artists would perform at the Flatland Picnic or if they didn't perform, they always showed up for support. This coupling kept Brookfield in the minds and hearts of those around Oakland.

The Williams family was responsible for most of the drugs circulating in the Oakland Flatlands and I grew up under the Williams' tutelage. Many people in the Jungle were envious of the Williams' success and money. But the Williams' was "bout it" (a term meaning ready for violence) and had a large crew. Other factions respected the Williams' enough to allow the Williams' to run most of the drugs for the Flatlands. The Williams' weren't invisible, they stayed on the same streets they served the drugs on.

Even though Brookfield had a lot of turfs (gang areas) in one, when there was funk (fighting) with other areas, we all came together as a single clan. However, when it came to hustling (making money illegally), every block had to hold their own.

The Flatlands made most of its money by local dealers selling marijuana and cocaine. This was done in front of many structures but mostly in front of storefronts, which turned storefronts into rough spots. There were dudes on Douglas Ave trying to sell heroin and the rest of the blocks sold cocaine. Usually, when one block was preferred to buy drugs from the others were too hot with police presence. Police would perform raids or issue injunctions. The D.E. and storefronts were competing points to make drugs sales for local dealers. They would compete against each other as far as who had the best quality rock or the most rock for the dollar. This type of sales competition kept the police performing weekly raids to curb drug sales. Each area of the Flatlands took turns serving drugs, which allowed the Flatlands to run like a well-oiled machine. When one end was hot from police activity, the drug users were ushered to the other end.

Our next-door hood, "across the tracks," as we referred to it, was Sobrante Park. It was one of the most dangerous and well-known turfs in Oakland. The two areas were only literally separated by train tracks. The two hoods (areas of town) had a real resentment for each other. However, the two hoods would rarely get out of hand and go to war with each other. It would usually only escalate to fist fights here and there.

As kids, we had to go to a middle school in Sobrante Park called Madison Elementary School. Sobrante Park had an elementary school called Sobrante Park Elementary and our local school was called Brookfield Elementary. The main high school everyone went to was called Castlemont High School. Castlemont is where most of the East Oakland gangs bonded and formed stronger unions. This was because other gangs attended. The outsider faction that attended our school usually looked at both of our factions, Sobrante Park and Brookfield, as common enemies based on the number of us in attendance at the school and our geographical location. These other neighborhoods were called the 80's, the 70's, and the 69th Village and 65th Village. Again, Brookfield is where I'm from.

The D.E.'s was pulling in lots of money at this time. One of the older persons that I looked up to took me to a house where they kept kilos of cocaine. His name was Taj and he asked me to help break cocaine kilos down into smaller packages for sale. This was the process for making volume sales out of mass weight. When performing this task, I was given around an ounce of crack cocaine to sell for my efforts. This translated into around $250 worth of crack rocks. It wasn't all packaged for small sales, it was all in quarter ounce chips. I would have to break the rocks down into smaller pieces for customers. I wanted all the money I could make, so instead of making all $25 crack pieces, I made them bigger and would only ask for $30 for the bigger pieces. It was good for me either way because I had no out of the pocket expense. The actual sale of the drug fascinated me and the money was just a plus. I loved to be viewed by the older people as a young man making his way.

When you sell crack, you have to adopt a different set of tactics not to get caught. I would go to the liquor store and buy a 50-cent razor and break it to expose the bare blade. I needed it to be new and sharp so it wouldn't shred the crack when I cut it. If the liquor store had a box of straight razors, it made the job a lot easier. Straight razors were the best tool when you had a purer crack that tended to be harder than the stuff that had a lot of cut. I would also buy from the store a $3 box of Glad sandwich bags. The bags had a double layer at the bottom, which made the crack rocks look bigger. The art of selling crack is all about the size for the money. The bigger the rocks look, the more eager a purchaser will be. Some sandwich bags didn't have the double layer at the bottom and they actually made the rocks look smaller. Once everything was in hand, I would head home and go in the bath-room, first stopping in the kitchen to grab a large plate. The bathroom was the safest place to be without prying eyes. The amount of time it would take me to bag everything up depended on the amount of crack I had. If it was an ounce of crack, it would usually take me around 45 minutes to cut and bag everything up. Out of each ounce of crack, I would usually cut about around $1600 worth of crack rocks. With only a $450 investment per ounce, this was a way of almost tripling my money with each investment. When I was done, I had around 160 rocks valued at $10 a piece. The whole thing looked like a large bag of jelly beans.

I would then take my bag full of rocks and head back to the liquor store. The doorway of this liquor store is usually where I would make the most money selling crack. I had a good rapport with the clerk of the store, so I really didn't have to worry about him calling the cops. We had our issues, of course, but overall we were cool. All he asked of me was that I kept a lot of people from hanging out in the doorway. I was basically his security guard, standing post while secretly making crack sales. To keep my crack sales out of the clerk's eyes, I developed a method for my transactions. I would reach out as if I were shaking someone's hand while passing over the crack rock; in another motion, I would then reach back with my free hand and grab the money. In my right pocket, I kept small bags full of $10 rocks and in the left $20 rocks. Depending upon what they asked for I would reach in either pocket to complete the sale. I was so consistent with the size and quality of the crack I had that the crack addicts trusted and respected me. They would take whatever it was I handed them without having to look at it or question it. I truly felt that I treated my customers good and always with respect.

The best thing you could do as a crack dealer was establish a great relationship with crack addicts; it kept me safe. I didn't look at them as less than human as some people did. Most addicts loved me for that acknowledgment. I never hit them or called them names. It was good and clean business, in my opinion. Being cool with them brought me benefits and advantages others didn't have. They would spend all of their money with me, even seek me out when at least 10 other people were standing on the block with crack. They would also warn me of when the police were coming. This gave me time enough to get away and stash my product. Some of them even would let me hide in their house as I was still on the run for violating probation. Yet there were times when it got really weird at some of their homes, well a lot of times actually.

I remember when this small skinny man who reminded me of Richard Pryor (the actor and comedian) moved into the corner house on Edes street. It took a few weeks for him to settle in. Eventually, I think he felt confident enough to want to get high and walked around looking to purchase some crack. He approached me out of the crowd of people standing near the corner, "Hey, would you follow me to my house for more privacy?"

I didn't think anything of it. This question was sort of typical for some people that lived close to my street. I followed him to his house and he purchased some crack from me. I noticed that he lived alone in a lovely home. I asked him if I could use his place to cut up my drugs, if it was all right with him. I guess he figured it was an easy way for him to get high. See, when you sold crack out of someone's house a small fee is paid, usually around $20 a day. It was called a "house fee." The house would also double down as a safe stash spot. On top of granting access to his home, he mentioned that he wanted to spend hundreds of dollars every time he bought something to get high on. We quickly formed a bond.

One day I went over there and he had prostitutes at the house. I wasn't shocked or angry about it. After all, it was his house, right? But then the next time I came over, he had a couple of my partners (associates from my area) in there with him. That made me upset! It was my hiding spot and I didn't need other people in there looking around at what I had built. Also, he was giving the money to them he was supposed to spend with me. Later on, that night after everyone had left, I had to give him a piece of my mind. He seemed receptive, so I left for the night.

The next day I went over there and a light-skinned, skinny dude was present. He wore a wave cap on his head. His look reminded me of the R&B singer Maxwell. The odd part was the way they interacted with each other. They would laugh and joke while they rubbed each other faces. It was as if a light bulb went off in my head, "These dudes are gay!" But then I thought, "Why are you tripping?" Cause the only thing I needed to be concerned about was my money. I had no problem with their sexual preferences as long as they didn't direct them toward me. One of my girlfriends was in hand with me. It was nothing serious, just someone with whom to spend time. I intended to take her in one of the rooms and have sex with her. I guess the homeowner knew what I was up to. He spoke in a deep hushed tone and said, "Can I watch?" I really wanted to cuss him out, but what was more critical was securing the spot to make money. I said, "Hell no," and headed to the room with her in tow. I guess I was a little nervous because it was over before you knew it. That was it and I escorted her home. It was a little weird after I figured out his sexual prefer-ence. Now that his secret was out, he no longer hid conversations from me. He would have openly gay conversations in my pres-ence. But this didn't deter me from going over there and making my money.

He owned a 1980 Mercedes Benz, a 4-door car model, burgundy in color. It was one of the old school designs that I really liked. One day he didn't have any money and wanted to get high. I asked if I could rent the car for the day in exchange for some crack. He agreed but told me that it needed gas. So I took it to the gas station and filled up the tank with unleaded fuel. My destination was my girlfriend's house but halfway there the car kept stalling and cutting off. Luckily there was a gas station at the next corner, into which I pulled the vehicle. Once at the gas station, I looked to see if the gas was low. It wasn't. I was confused as far as what could be wrong with the car. Scratching my head, I looked over the Mercedes walking around it and noticed on the gas tank lid it said, "Powered by diesel fuel." I had no idea what that meant and kept trying to start the car until the battery died. I spent most of the day trying to find someone to jump the battery. When this was successful, it would only run for a few minutes and then die again. The last time I got it jumped the car ran for 5 minutes before it ultimately died. I was lucky to make it back to Brookfield with the car cutting off and on. At his home, I let him know what was going on. He said to me, "You can't put unleaded gas in a diesel fuel injected vehicle. Now I got to get the gas tank drained for it to run right."

I said, "Sorry bro," reaching into my pocket and handing him some crack. Continuing, "I hope this is enough for my mistake," giving him about $30 total worth of crack. He nodded and that was the end of that. I continued to go over to his house daily and make money when it was available to be made.

I was actually making good money each day and felt a lot safer than standing out on the street selling drugs. On this one day as I had just finished cutting up about $500 worth of crack into small crack rocks. I was trying to be slick and stash it in a room cabinet that looked inaccessible. In my mind, I was sure he wouldn't find my stash. What I didn't consider was that someone on crack can smell it when they fiend for it. Their nose can pinpoint where it is. Or maybe they are just lucky at finding dope. It's part of their tweak to look around as if they dropped some dope on the ground. So after the evening was setting in and I came back to the house to get some rocks out of my stash, I saw it was all gone! I wasn't into hurting people behind drugs, but I had to at least scare this guy. I tried to scare him into giving my money back by making threats towards him. He agreed and said to give him a couple of days to get the money.

I felt confident that my threats had worked. I felt confident until the day came when it was time for him to pay me. I tried the doorknob, but it was locked. I stood there and knocked on the door. No answer. I knocked harder this time hoping he was only in the bathroom and possibly didn't hear me. Still no response. I stood at the door at least 45 minutes pounding on it, knowing he had to be somewhere in the house. Then something told me to look in the window. When I did, the house was empty. I guess this guy figured it was time for him to move on. It shook me a little and made me feel really stupid.

✖ ✖ ✖

I had time to recover and was building a close bond with Taj. What Taj, this older individual, did was distribute crack cocaine for sale to various people that were trusted in the neighborhood. This enabled many people that had nothing, no upfront capital, to earn an income.

Most people that sell crack never transform cocaine into rock. The process involves a beaker, powder cocaine, and baking soda. First, you pour the powder cocaine into a beaker. Next, place the beaker into a pot of boiling water, allowing the cocaine to melt from the heat. Then you pour whatever amount of baking soda you'd like into the liquefied cocaine. It's usually a ratio of 1 ounce of cocaine to a half ounce of baking soda. Other people used other additives to cut the cocaine, like B12 powder or procaine. How strong the crack turns out really depends on the cook, but you did have to keep in mind how much cut, whether baking soda or another additive, you mixed in. If you added too much baking soda your final crack rock would be soft and tend to melt if too much heat is applied to it, whether it be body heat or from the heat of the day. Once you add the baking soda, it dissolves and absorbs into the cocaine. The mixture looks like clear jello sitting in water. You then swirl the beaker around allowing the mixture to properly blend. The mixing of the ingredients takes only about 30 seconds. You then remove the beaker from the pot of boiling water allowing it to cool. Some people used bowels of ice to rapidly cool the mixture. Once everything cools, it solidifies and will form a solid rock in the bottom of the beaker. It usually takes around 10 minutes to get hard. Finally, you just use a butter knife or any other sharp object to remove the wafer-like cookie from the bottom. The amount you can cook at one time depended on the size of the beaker. Although I have never cooked cocaine into crack, I have seen it done many times.

Like every other crack spot, after a while, the police move into a new area from which they received too many calls about drugs sales or shootings. As summer was getting hot, Brookfield cooled off. D.E. was the latest spot that had revenue coming in. It made many people that viewed the D.E. as an area that you couldn't make money in, differently. The D.E. had only been slow due to police activity. People started to once again frequent the D.E. This was a plus for me because very few people envied me now as I was selling in Brookfield. This gave me an advantage in selling drugs.

Selling crack can be stressful for some dealers. I have seen people drink, for peace of mind, the entire time they are selling. Others will sit and smoke weed all day while on the block, to calm their nerves. I, however, needed nothing for my conscience. I witnessed it being used in my home so much that crack use was second nature to me. The difference that paused me was I really couldn't keep putting myself on the frontline selling drugs due to the constant undercover raids. Also, there was so much crack in the neighborhood, it made everyone rush potential crack sale customers. Meaning as soon as one customer drove up there would be three to four people running up to the car with crack rocks for sale. If you didn't have the biggest rocks or weren't fast enough, you'd miss out on each sale that came through.

I supplemented my income shooting dice. Dice games shot anywhere from $5-$20 a roll. Side bets kept the pot growing bigger each time. On the streets, there was a sense of family with everyone enjoying making money and blasting music all day and night long. The experience was fun for an upcoming teenager selling crack.

The downside about the drug game was if it was a slow night, you can stand out in the cold all night long to make pocket change. And with your older homie providing you the drugs and eating off of what you make, it could get frustrating. Still, as soon as it seemed like everything was coming to a standstill, something would break open and people would get paid and there would be plenty of money for everyone again. The thing that kept you out of jail was your patience and your willingness to wait until things picked up. If not you'd likely rush a sale and it'd be an under-cover cop.

✖ ✖ ✖

Throughout my drug sales career, I had many situations of being stolen from. The way it happened was always differ-ent. It usually occurred like a magic act, in a snap of the fingers. One occasion, in particular, occurred after I got out of the shower. I needed one as I had been out most of the night making money. After my shower, I decided to go back out to get rid of the rest of the rocks I had. I put my clothes on but forgot to grab the money I had on the bathroom counter. As soon as I made it to the front door, it dawned on me; I thought, "Oh yeah, let me grab the money I left." I quickly dashed back to the bathroom, but my two aunties and dad were in the house. I hoped it wasn't gone. See, two minutes had passed, an eternity for cash laying around, but I still had to look. Walking into the bathroom, of course, it was gone and I had no idea who was to blame for the theft. I walked into the living room and asked, with a snarl on my face, "Who the hell took my money from the bathroom?" Who got my money?" I was talking loudly, almost to the point of yelling, and I was looking as mean and mad as I could. My aunt shocked me and said, "Don't be yelling in grandma's house!" Once she said that I knew it was her. I was furious, so I grabbed her and slapped her. It was getting more serious by the second. My other aunt jumped up and got between us. I couldn't press my slapped aunt for information on my money anymore because she wasn't going for it. Then my cousin spoke up as if to intervene. Before he could really say anything, I got in his face. I walked through the entire house asking anyone and everyone if they saw my money. I even begged my grandma to refund me like the good old days, when she would replace things that I lost in her house. But granny said, "Now you know how I feel about you losing stuff."

Truthfully I had no idea who took my money and by the guilty party knowing this, they'd never admit to it. I ended up without my cash. Luckily I still had about $1,000 worth of crack rocks. I was forced to start all over again. One of the things I remember most was every time I would take a loss like that I would be harder on the grind trying to make money.

Even so, I was reckless with all the money I made. I would buy cars for around $1200 or $1000 and lose them 10 minutes later in a dice game. Or I left them, engine running on the street, by bailing out and fleeing when the police got behind me. Remember, I was still on the run for a probation violation and had no license. Then I'd go right back on the grind and rebuild my money. I lost $800 shooting dice one day and had recovered my losses by the end of the night. During this time, money would vary. It could take a couple of nights or sometimes only one night to make thousands of dollars selling crack. All it depended on was how the block was rolling and how many customers came by. Selling dope was a job to me. I didn't have any other responsibilities other than securing my money. My days were grinding on the block.

During this time, I ran into another O.G that I admired. His name was K.K. He located me on the block as I was hopping out of a black Ford Explorer, trying to make some money. He had heard of all the money I was making for Taj. K.K. approached me and asked, "What's up, Drew?" I was really excited that he knew who I was. He followed up, "Do you want to grind (sell drugs)?" I immediately replied, "Hell yeah!" He nodded his head and said, "Instead of what Taj is giving you, I'm going to give you wholes (whole ounces) instead of quarter pieces." A smile as big as Texas spread across my face. I replied, "Hell Yeah, I'm ready to move up and step up my position in the Brook" (nickname for Brookfield.) I knew that Taj wouldn't mind. He was the O.G. on the block and had plenty of people working for him. When Taj would drop off my sack of rocks for the day, he had three other people there getting the same issue if not more.

At this time, the Flatlands began to make money again. In the eyes of those around me, I was established as being solid (not a snitch) and I felt it was my turn to make real money. "K" was the person in charge of running the block, and I was going to be his prodigy. With the high quality of cocaine that I now had, I would sell out very quickly. It began to become as soon as the drugs touched my hands, they were gone. Money was rolling in and people had started to notice me. The Flatlands began to ringing in people's minds as being the place to be at. K used to pick me up daily and ride around town with me. He would call me by my real name real loud so that people around would know that I was his "youngin." I guess that was a way to keep people from trying to rob me.

K adapted the nickname "Rider" for me. The name came from me always being energized and ready for anything. We already had an O.G. in the hood named Rider, but I guess that was overlooked by many as I was young and making my way. The new nickname slid right in and fit me to a tee. Being on the block and hanging around K formed a new identity for me.

I took the name Rider and wore it as a badge. But with the new identity came new challenges. I felt as if I needed to become active in the art of pistol play now. Which meant that if necessary, I needed to shoot people to live up to my new nickname. So that's what I did.

Anytime there was an issue or unresolved problem, I wanted to be the first to respond. This new ego played tricks on my mind. It gave me a false sense of being a God. The other downside about hanging around with killers is you learn to devalue life.

I had more money than I knew what to do with and the peers around me loved me. I bought 6 gold teeth to put in my mouth and went crazy on tattoos, getting 7 of them in one session. I now owned cars and had stylish clothes to wear. I also had a street block to call my own. My identity of me being a rider took me to new heights I could have never before imagined.

RIDER VERSUS LITTLE ANDREW

My new identity of Rider was that of a young boy trying to prove himself in a world of adults. While my "Little Andrew" persona seemed to be drowned out more every day. I would do almost anything to prove my allegiance and lack of conscience. There were things (deep down) I did not like doing, like robbing and stealing. I really had no reason to participate other than the thrill of the crime. Robbing was unnecessary. I was making good money selling crack. But if I saw someone not from Brookfield trying to set up shop, I had to take him down.

It was an easy process, all I needed to do was walk up to the person and offer to smoke some weed with him. Once he didn't visualize a threat, the heist was easy. Once, I eased toward a guy that wasn't from around the area. I offered to smoke weed with him and he agreed. I pulled out a baggie of some good marijuana and rolled it up. Lighting it, I could see how eager he was to smoke. We passed the marijuana joint back and forth a few times. I only took small hits and he drew in large deep pulls of the pungent weed. As I saw the drug taking its effect on him, I quickly pulled my pistol and made him empty his pockets. It was only a few dollars and about 5 $10 crack rocks. The point wasn't to use the proceeds to make me rich; it was to show outsiders that if you weren't from the block, you couldn't make money here. I also didn't like going to other people neighborhoods. I was pretty sure they would do the same thing to me.

Gang banging had its own set of problems. It would turn into me having issues with people I was cool with just because one of my homeboys got into it with them. But the unwritten rule was you always chose the homeboys over, whether they were right or wrong, over any other faction. My crew was the people I hung out with every day and there was rarely a situation where I had problems of my own. My troubles came from the egos of those around me.

Compared to Rider, Lil Andrew was genuinely smiling all the time. He was polite and would say, "Excuse me" when passing someone. Lil Andrew was always thoughtful and said, "Thank you" or "You're welcome," when appropriate. Being Lil Andrew required me to transform from street savvy Rider into a man with a conscience. While home, I would keep the drugs, money, and the guns hidden. It was as if I were two different people: a Doctor Jekyll and Mr. Hyde in real life.

I would enjoy spending time with my family as Lil Andrew. It was the Oscar-winning role of my life playing like Lil Andrew was the only side of me. My grandparents knew that I was hanging out on the corner, but thought I was just hanging out. See, they had never seen me

selling drugs. As Lil Andrew, I loved going to the recreational center or the Boys Club. I also frequented local parks, basically anything positive to create some balance in my life.

As Rider, I only liked hanging out on the block and places where gang members hung out at. Rider continued to gain fame in the eyes of those on the block. Lil Andrew was a servant to his grandparents, cutting their grass and cleaning the house. Things Rider would never do. Rider was too focused on making money and earning a street reputation.

I enjoyed the new experience of high school, but I couldn't stay long. I had money to make. I would check into school for a couple hours and then ditch the rest of the day. I would also frequent other high schools just to see if there was money to be made selling crack and, of course, to see the girls. In school or while outside, where thugs would gather was where Rider felt at home. Castlemont High is the place where Rider showed out the most. Rider was a person that reacted on impulse.

One day I was walking around school and I noticed a handful of homies huddled around a guy named Keen. They were all in fighting stances ready to jump him. As Rider, I came in next to the fight while I hyped up the crowd. The crazy part was that Keen and I were friends in junior high, but this was high school. So, as I saw them all squaring off, without thinking, I blasted Keen in the eye. I assumed the rest of the people would finish him off (protocol in a street fight) but instead of following protocol, everyone stood there. I ended up fighting Keen by myself.

I always seemed to do silly impulsive things like that all the time. It usually meant that I ended up getting all the drama to deal with by myself also; which often meant I was dealing with somebody else's issues. The reality is that's what usually happens when you put your nose in someone else's business.

Lil Andrew was different, he just wanted to eat sweets and laugh all day long. He had a passion for playing video games, also. All in all, Lil Andrew really didn't get any attention. This was unless it was to be his service of cleaning up the house or to run errands for Granny or Grandpa. Then he also had to give Granny massages to get the cramps out of her aching body.

While Rider was accepted by all because he would do what others weren't brave enough to do, or were smart enough not to do, Lil Andrew was shy and alone. I needed love and attention from my peers, so I did what I did to keep them needing me. This was until I started getting older and more established on the block. That was the time I believe I removed Lil Andrew all together from my mind. Only then was I able to slow down and relax. After coming up, I didn't have to be so eager to impress those around me. I was no longer considered the youngster, but now an older homie.

The stakes were higher with this new designation. The conflicts that I was involved in were more dangerous. These conflicts usually amounted to gunplay, which meant someone was going to die. I was eager but still thought that actions had no real consequences. At least this was what every rap song or gangster movie I watched displayed. I once again began to incorporate some of this fiction into my real life. I made my circle of people that I hung around into those that were known killers in the neighborhood. People would see the crowd I frequented and tell me to stay away. I, of course, never listened, and thought they were trying to control my life. In addition, the killers that I hung around showed me love (embraced me), so I felt like a part of something. I was now seen riding around town with these dudes daily. By doing so, I would get acknowledged by people from whom I least expected it. This band of killers treated me as if I grew up with them, treating me like family. As time went on, they became familiar with the ego of Rider.

Sometimes I would see older dudes around Oakland and get greeted as if I was a celebrity. There was nothing but love that came my way. I started feeling like I was a factor that made a difference. In truth, I was only a factor because of the violence I was willing to commit. I was a participant in the street life and the destruction of those that opposed me. Since this type of behavior made me acknowledged by all, I took it to another excessive level.

Violence became an addiction to me. However, because of the violence I enacted, an invisible target was placed on my back; one that made me fear going home at times. I would just go by the house and check in on my grandparents to keep them from getting mad at me. If I didn't check in, when I would show up there would be hours of yelling and questioning by my grand-parents.

When these situations occurred, I would wait on them to go to sleep and just climb out my bedroom window. My destination was the block and I would stay there until around 3 a.m. I would then go back home by climbing back through the window, take a quick nap, and be up by 6 a.m., ready to go and do it all over again. All it required was me putting my pants back on, rolling up a blunt (a marijuana-laced cigar), washing my face, and brushing my teeth and hair. This was my morning ritual and then right back to the block again. In my mind, I would think that I was missing money if I did anything else. I was addicted to hustling and it had its grips on me tough. See, it was more than just the money, but the whole exchange that was the icing on the cake. The game was played as such - I give you a few crack rocks and you place a few bills in my hand. If you want to spend $100 or more and I didn't have it on me at the time, well, you could give me a ride to my house, or wait in the front of the store and I would provide you with whatever you needed. The product was the best around.

MY COMMITMENT OFFENSE

I t was now the early part of the year 2000. Things were going as well as I expected them to with me making money. I was established and loved by all around me. At this time, my uncle got out of prison. I didn't get to spend much time with my uncle before he went to prison. But now I was 16 years old and he was 31 years old. He didn't view me as a kid anymore. He quickly picked up where he left off at. He came by one day and we took a drive. I loved riding around in his car. It was a root beer brown 1988 Chevy Nova with flashy rims and the latest sound system. We spent the time making small talk. He basically gave me my accolades on what I had accomplished street wise since he been gone. He told me that he had plans to take over and sew up the Brookfield cocaine game. I quickly thought, "He's planning to take over the drug game I'm already established in?" But since he was my uncle, my thoughts were, "Cool."

I was sort of trying to duck K.K., not that I owed him anything, but we had a good rapport with each other. I finally ran into him one day. I could see the look of disappointment on his face. We were at a party and I was hanging out with my uncle. I was with my uncle in a dark corner of the house. K.K. approached us and pulled me to the side. All he said was, "See!" As if warning me about hanging with thugs. There was no real bad blood between K.K. and me, he just felt he had taught me better than that.

After K.K. made his way, I walked back over to my uncle and he asked if I would recruit a couple of members. I really didn't like the concept of them just moving in and taking over, but I agreed. I went back to the block and found 6 dudes that I felt were trustworthy. One of them was Antonio. I always knew Antonio since we were younger. Antonio sort of voiced his opinion that he didn't want to fully commit to my uncle and what my uncle had going on, but he would support me. This was due to his baby's mamma being my cousin. This made Antonio feel somewhat comfortable that he would roll with us.

My uncle came by the house one day with a big plastic bag full of quarter ounces of cocaine. He said he would give me and all the recruits a quarter ounce of crack just for being on his team. I guess it was an incentive for being recruited. The free ounce didn't have to be repaid. He said, "Just make sure that after you get rid of the product, you come to me for future supplies."

I had enough customers regularly coming that I needed around 1 to 2 ounces of crack daily. And what my uncle was proposing was that we all buy only in quarter ounces at $150 each. That deal would leave me little room for profit as my average purchase was around $1200 for bulk. But I assumed this was his way of recruiting so I took the product from him and moved on.

In Brookfield, all of the other dudes that were already established selling crack sort of fell back. I don't know if they felt something or had heard something in the wind. I say this because the overall vibe was no one wanted violence to occur in the neighborhood. They knew me to be a violent person and rightfully assumed my crew was also.

Time can be both your enemy and your friend. It didn't take long for us to take over the drug trade in Brookfield. I no longer needed anyone for my drugs because my uncle had it for me. It became very dangerous with that position on the streets; which made me the prey for all that was around. But I honestly felt safe in everything I did.

My uncle was becoming a household name, as his crew was making good money now. We threw lavish parties for all to come and attend. There were giant bottles of Remy Martin for all to drink. The parties had all the weed you could smoke as we provided ounces of top-grade marijuana. We also had pills for all that popped them. We supplied everything free of charge.

By this time, I felt like I was on top of the world. I had a vicious crew and all of them had my back. I trusted them by proxy because my uncle was the leader of the crew and it seemed that everyone involved came to me for decisions. I would help them in deciding whether violence was necessary or not depending on the situation.

✖ ✖ ✖

We were all on the block just hanging out on this particular day. Antonio had called my uncle while we were there and said he was on his way, not to go anywhere. I guess to recoup (obtain more crack.) I didn't ask why he called. My uncle did say Antonio said it would take around 10 minutes as he was coming from Dag. He had to drive over the ramp that connected Dag to the Flatlands. When Antonio finally made it, my uncle and me, along with a few crew members, were sitting in a black Mercedes Benz. Antonio walked up to the car and saw all of us there. Instead of getting in the car, he just nodded as if to say what's up and he kept walking.

Immediately following his departure, a yellow car pulled up. They didn't say anything but started shooting at us and the vehicle we were sitting in. Everyone in the car ducked down to use the car to shield ourselves from the flying bullets. I couldn't see anything other than the windshield shattering from the bullets that hit. I could also hear the thud of bullets against the side of the car. One end of the car dropped when a bullet hit the tire bursting it. After a matter of seconds, it grew eerily quiet. I heard the tires of the other car squeal as the driver hit the gas pedal for them to flee the scene. I popped my head up and looked around. Everyone sort of sat there motionless looking at each other. We all slowly rose up and exited the car. The windshield was gone and there were bullet holes up the side of the vehicle. The smell of burnt gun powder was still fresh in the air. Whoever was shooting was a very poor shot. Most of the bullets were on the front side of the car with only a couple hitting the door.

Things were going smooth until the day we got ambushed. Luckily no one was hit, but this changed everything. As I sat in the car, I understood that violence and gunplay will forever be closely intertwined with the drug game, but that didn't make what happened an easy pill to swallow.

In the days following the drive-by shooting, my uncle was livid. He went crazy saying, "It's on as soon as you see anyone not in our crew!" This was to be our retaliation for the shooting. Our next move was riding around Brookfield, shooting at people in different areas. We even went to different neighborhoods looking for people that might be responsible for the drive-by. Then one day my uncle came over. I could see the look of fire in his eyes. He said, "I think 'Tone' (Antonio) was paid to set the whole thing up. It's his words that triggered the hit on my crew."

This enraged me because I felt betrayed. It also turned into a feeling of fear because now I felt vulnerable as I had brought

Tone into the crew. For Tone to put my life in jeopardy left me in a feeling of rage. My uncle held it as something that had to be taken care of and I, of course, felt compelled to take care of it.

✖ ✖ ✖

After the failed hit on the crew and the notion that it was Antonio, I took it upon myself to go on a solo mission to find Antonio. But searching for him proved difficult as he seemed to have disappeared. I finally was able to locate him one night. It was now August 16th, 2001. I had just made it home after a day of spending money at the mall on new clothes and shoes. I looked at the clock on the stove and it said 10:30 p.m. My grandmom noticed me in the house. She came out of her room and said, "Boy, you know it's late. Why don't you just go in your room and lay down."

I replied, "I'll be back in 30 minutes Granny. I just got one more run to make." She replied, "All right boy, but you're pushing it."

I quickly went to my room and grabbed my gun. Leaving home without my pistol left me feeling naked. I went outside and headed down to the block. As soon as I made it, I did my usual scan of the surroundings. It was as if a beacon of light lit up. I noticed Antonio standing there alone, brushing his fingers through his dreadlocks. He was dressed in all black. He noticed me as I approached him. When I made it to where he was standing a smile spread across his face. We embraced each other as if we were longtime friends. After making small talk about the things that occurred in the past year, I grew impatient. Here standing before me was this dude that tried to kill me and was now acting as if nothing ever happened.

I asked him, "Do you want to go and look for the dudes that had shot at our crew?"

He replied, "Let's do this," lifting up his shirt to display his pistol. This was his way of showing me that he was prepared. Honestly, a million thoughts were running through my head. I thought about all that I had been through and where I was now headed.

✕ ✕ ✕

On August 16th, 2001, at around 11:30 p.m., Antonio Young and I were walking down the street. It had been a year since I had last seen him. The smell of gun powder still filled my nostrils, from the day he tried to have me killed. Even though there was no concrete proof of Antonio being the orchestrator, he was rumored to have been the person responsible for setting up the crew and attempting to have us murdered. It wasn't as if I could just let him go as if nothing had happened, but I was caught off guard because he had a pistol on him also. I had to plan the shooting without allowing him to shoot back. There was no doubt in my mind that he would kill if he had to.

What I devised was that he couldn't shoot if his gun was open. I asked him to show me the bullets in his gun. I remember he used to brag about using hollow points. He smiled and nodded his head. I began to walk away from the corner where we stood, leading Antonio to an empty street. As soon as he opened his chamber to his pistol, I quickly drew and shot him 5 times. One of the bullets hit him in the face, two rounds hit him in the arm, and two entered his back, as he turned trying to flee. He crumpled down to the ground. As he laid there, I turned and ran. As soon as I turned the corner, I encountered the surprise of my life.

As I was making my exit, I was immediately noticed by an unmarked police car that was headed in my direction. Since I was wearing all white, it was easy for them to see me. I was already out of breath and frantic with fear and anxiety. I guess a call went out that shots were fired in the area. The cops immediately slammed on the brakes to the car and hopped out with guns drawn. One of them yelled, "Hey!" I immediately took off running. I dashed down an alley and threw the gun I still had in my possession in the bushes. I kept running until I reached this house from which we sold drugs. I went to the rear of the house and banged on the window. The woman that lived in the house looked out the window and saw me standing there. She came around and let me in. The weirdest part of the situation was she didn't ask me any questions, but just went to her room to continue getting high.

I sat in the house, now trapped. My heart pounded so hard I thought it would pop through my chest. I could hear the OPD helicopter whirling above. I could see the high beam light on the helicopter circle all around the area. There was no place to go. What I didn't know was that the police had seen me go in the house. They soon had the house surrounded with guns drawn. A detective came to the door and the lady of the house went and opened the door for them. I was detained without further incident.

While riding in the police car, I was thinking, "What the hell went so wrong so quickly?" I was nervous and truly felt like my life was over. We arrived at the police station. I was removed from the car and taken into the interrogation room. In this room, I was handcuffed to a table. I sat at this table for a while waiting on someone to enter. It felt like days sitting there. Someone finally entered the room. I asked, "How long have I been here." The detective told me, "You've been here since 2 a.m. Just relax and we'll get to you shortly." He showed me his watch and I was shocked that 12 hours had passed while I was sat in the interrogation room. I hadn't had anything to eat or drink the whole time. He took me over to the desk to be fingerprinted and photographed. I was then booked into jail.

The hardest part of the event that had transpired was I had a phone call to make. I had to call home and let them know where I was. My father answered the phone on the second ring. It crushed me to tell him where I was and what I was up against. When he asked me what did they pick me up for? I replied, "Murder!" I had never felt so defeated in my life. Here I sat in jail with no idea of how they figured it was me that did the shooting or if they in-fact knew it was me that did it. I was sure no one was in the alley and saw what occurred.

I sat in the holding cell most of the night. In the early morning, a detective came to the cell and told me that I would be transferred to the Juvenile Detention Center. I was transported late on August 17th. Juvenile Hall was where I would be appropriately housed because I was only 16 years old at the time and couldn't be housed in the county jail pending trial.

While sitting at the facility awaiting trial, my mind raced daily. I went over every mistake I had made and regretted all of them. I had no energy and slept most of the days that passed. I had grown accustomed to being around older individuals and now being trapped in a facility with people my age made me feel even more out of place.

✖ ✖ ✖

I stayed at this juvenile facility until I was 18. There was no need to rush into the trial. My lawyer agreed that by waiving time, it could help him investigate the prosecutor's evidence and build a defense. When I turned 18, the juvenile jail chose to send me to the local county jail. The county jail was much different from the juvenile housing facility. It was nothing but grown men in there. Most of them were drug addicts, but there were some gang members also. I didn't know who my friends were or who was my enemy. It was a situation in which I didn't trust anybody.

I have a large frame and carried my weight well. This gave me an advantage against people trying to pick on me. Not to mention, I was highly aggressive and would fight with anyone I felt threatened by. My rage would be usually centered on those that provoked me. It was as if I was genuinely spiraling out of control. I wasn't big on talking and thought that I would let my hands speak for me.

The trial finally came. There were no more reasons to buy time. The judge wouldn't allow it. I was still in denial about my culpability in what occurred. In my mind, it was Antonio's fault for what had happened. When I talked about the incident to anyone, it would anger me when someone didn't take my point of view on the event. My excuse was, "He tried to set us up and get us killed!" Others held so many notions about what happened and also what should have happened. Their ideas only furthered my anger. The way I saw it, people didn't know what happened, yet everyone had a story to tell about me.

In court, I was angry the entire time. I was in denial and blaming Antonio for making me do it. I really had no defense other than it wasn't me.

While Antonio's mother didn't attend most of the trial, one day she was supposed to come and testify. On the day she was supposed to show up, the D.A. said that she submitted the following letter to the court:

> "To whomever reads this letter, I really don't know where to begin. Life has been very hard for me since August 17, 2001. This is the day that because of the decision made by Andrew, my life changed forever. Not only did I lose my first born, I also lost my unborn child.
>
> For years I prayed to be able to get my life together so that I could be there to enjoy life with my children. I want you to

know in the year 1999 I did just that. I became the mom I should've been all along. And I was very happy being with my kids and new granddaughter. I couldn't have ever been happier. All of my kids are very special to me. Each in their own little way.

Antonio was my sunshine!! I can remember many days I was scared, sad, and depressed. Changing wasn't as easy as it seemed. But lo and behold Antonio was right there. Encouraging and strengthening me. No matter how sad and depressed I was, he could make all that go away in a matter of seconds. He kept me laughing and smiling.

He was also always a big help when it came to his younger brothers. He always told me, "Mom it's gonna be all right. I'll always be here to help you with my brothers." And they loved and respected him more than words can ever explain. He was all they had. There was never another male figure that meant that much to them. He was their mornings and nights.

After his daughter was born, he seemed like the most happiest person in the world. She was his everything. Where ever he went she was right there with him. It was wonderful to see him smile the way he did when he looked at her. When he held her. When he simply talked to her. It was then I realized my son was the happiest man in the world. All he talked about was his daughter. But Andrew took all of this away.

I can never really explain in words how hurt I am. Still 3 years later I can't sleep or barely eat. Every day I ask myself over and over why Antonio? He never did anything in life to hurt anybody. He always wanted people to be happy. And believe me he worked overtime to make sure they were. It almost seemed like that was his purpose, to make people happy.

Not only did I lose my son and newborn, my son in school

went from being a straight A student graduating with honors (thank you Antonio) to a convicted felon. My 11-year old walks around all day being sad, crying for his older brother. This has affected us all tremendously. We never knew we would have to spend the rest of our lives without our sunshine. I was supposed to speak today, but my anger wouldn't let me.

You see the Wadsworths will always be able to write and talk to their son. They'll still be able to wish him a Merry X-mas or Happy Birthday by card or letter. I'll never again be able to enjoy those moments. All I have is a pile of dirt that represents my son. No address to send anything to.

I still remember the day Antonio introduced me to Andrew. He said, "Ma, meet my friend, Andrew." How can a friend take the life of another friend? Someone who cared about him as a brother? Antonio never brought anyone around me he did not consider a real friend. Never!!!

I don't know what else to say. All I can say is I hope for the rest of his natural life Andrew is held accountable for the decisions he made on August 17th. Because, I too am being punished."

I couldn't understand how this woman wanted to paint this picture of Antonio being such a good person. He tried to kill me. The jury must have read my anger and quickly returned with a guilty verdict. The judge asked before he pronounced a sentence, was there anything I wanted to say. With my foolish ego and anger, I choose to not say anything.

Today, in my mind, these words echo for Antonio:

"I am so sorry for the incident that occurred. For the act of possessing a gun and pulling the trigger that ended your life. I want to apologize to you and your family for the physical, mental, and spiritual pain I have caused.

For a long time, I was in denial about my actions of evil. However, as I took the time to reflect on me and put myself in your shoes, I have begun the process of maturing and becoming a different and better person. It starts with me holding myself accountable and taking full responsibility. I made a choice and doing so, I learned insight and the understanding of the impact I caused. Now, I can see clearly, without excuse and blame.

On August 16th, 2001 at 11 p.m. at night, I transformed into a monster in a real-life movie that victimized you and terrorized your family in ways only the devil can imagine and only God can bring healing to. I am sincerely sorry for my doings, from the center of my soul. For carrying out the devil's work and destroying God's hand-picked present that was put here for your family, your friends, and the community that loved you for 18 years.

I know apologizing will never bring you back, but I pray that turning my life around and making amends to your family, the youth, your daughter, and the world is a start. I plan to give back, whether it's directly, indirectly, or through prayer to "all" in need of positive reinforcement, so they'll at least have a fighting chance to overcome the negative. I plan to show the youth how not to make the choices I made and how to persevere with confidence in doing the right thing. Making the world and people to understand and think about consequences, before actions, is my plan.

Antonio, as long as I can work on myself (replacing bad for good) your passing will not go in vain. Even though you are in heaven, the youth, through me will remember your name, all due respect to you.

My motivation is changed. "No more tears, no more inflicting pain."

Instead of saying these words that have echoed in my head for years, I chose to say nothing. My reaction was a smirk on my face. I chose to allow my ignorance to overwhelm me and feel no remorse at the time. I was delusional and seriously thought that I was the real victim.

At the sentencing hearing, the judge asked if there was any litigating versus mitigating factors to be presented. My lawyer submitted a letter written to the court by Antonio's grandmother. It read as follows:

"I am Antonio's maternal grandmother. Antonio comes from a large family which you have seen here during trial and now. That family consists of his mother, his step-father, paternal grandmother, great grandmother, grandfather, aunts and uncles, great aunts and uncles, cousins, his girlfriend and mother of his child and her family, and friends. I had originally intended to share some of Antonio's life with you but whenever I tried to write about him, I found that I can only allow myself those memories in bits and pieces because the totality of them are still too painful to allow myself to feel. I'm sure that other family members have had the same problem in trying to write their letters to the Court for this hearing. So I've decided that Antonio's character and the love we shared with and for him speaks for itself by our presence here.

Instead, I'd like to address a few questions to Andrew Wadsworth. What happened between 1985, the year you were born, and August 16, 2001, just 16 years later? How did you go from a newborn baby, who I'm sure brought love, joy, and pride to your parents, family, and friends to a cold-blooded killer who now brings immeasurable hurt and anger to not only your family but Antonio's family also? What changed that "bundle of joy" in those 16 years that you could cold-bloodedly shoot down a young man who - in your own words - had never done anything to harm you? Never even had an argument with you? The same young man who you laughed with, shared ideas, dreams, and even jokes with? A young father with whom, a short year before, you shared his joy at the baby shower in anticipation of the pending birth of his child! What kind of person had you become in those 16 years that you could walk him down that dark street knowing that at the end of that walk you intended to shoot him down with less feeling than you would have for a stray dog? What kind of person did you become that when you drew your gun and he realized what was happening, and threw up his arms, the ONLY weapons he had to protect himself, you shot him in both arms (not where you intended I'm sure); then when he turned to run you shot him twice in the back; then as he lay fearfully on the ground, in pain and bleeding from his wounds, perhaps pleading but surely crying, you walked up to him and shot him point blank in the head?

Then you sat here through all the hearings, trial, and on the witness stand and attempted to convince this Court, the jurors, and our family that you were afraid for your life? That you shot him in self-defense? Antonio's character and reputation speaks to the person he is because surely if your attorney had been able to present Antonio in a different light, he would have, rather than the testimony you presented through your drug-addicted, prostitute cousin who sat on the witness stand and blatantly lied, and your own self-serving lies about what Antonio supposedly told you he had done in the past. In all Oakland, did no one else but the two of you know the Antonio you tried to present in this courtroom? And, as he lay bleeding, being questioned by the police officer about who shot him, and under the mistaken belief that he would be okay, I believe that again his character showed through in his refusal to give up your name as the person who shot him. Why? Not a spirit of being uncooperative with the police, but because he still considered you, Andrew, a friend! You yourself described the real Antonio when in response to the question that was asked of you while on the witness stand, you responded that "he wasn't that kind of guy, he didn't make trouble!"

Please tell me, what kind of human you became during those 16 short years? Who gave you the right to decide that my grandson's life should end on August 17, 2001? Well, I can't answer that question but I can tell you this; by your actions that night, you gave this Court the right to decide how you will live possibly for the rest of your life. In prison, locked up like the predator you are! And we hope it's for a very, very long time. No, this brings no joy to our family. Only a sense of justice served.

I must say to your family, however, that my sympathies go out to them for they are in an unenviable position. On the other hand, they still have the pleasure of seeing you, talking with you, watching you grow, maybe even touching, hugging you. But the saddest part of this entire ordeal is that Antonio's daughter will grow up without ever knowing her father other than through what others are able to tell her. A father who, you know from firsthand knowledge, absolutely adored his daughter and thought the sun rose and set on her!

One thing I am certain of though; I know where Antonio will spend eternity! Around the age of 12 or 13, much to my surprise, Antonio confessed Christ as his Lord and Savior! God moved his heart then because He knew that August 17, 2001 was coming. My final questions to you then Andrew Wadsworth: What's in your heart? Do you know where you will spend eternity? As children of God, and in obedience to our Lord and Savior, we have no choice but to forgive you. We all will also pray for you and your family because even with forgiveness, there are still consequences we must endure because of bad choices made and wrong paths walked. And when we leave here today, the real consequences for your bad choices will begin."

This was a very powerful and impactful statement. Remember I was still in full denial about my culpabilities in the crime at this time. I simply smirked and laughed while most of the letter was read. The judge sentenced me to 50 years to life. It really didn't bother me because I had felt that I had a life sentence coming regardless of what I said or did. As soon as the judge pronounced the verdict, the family of Antonio started smiling and clapping. I would never let them see me sweat and turned around and smiled at them as I was being escorted out of the courtroom. Another foolish decision I made that I regret to this day.

I was transported back to the county jail. That night I called home to let my family know what happened. For the first time, I felt sorrow and regret. I cried as I told my grandmom what had happened. They had no idea what had occurred as I had told my family to stay home during the trial.

MY NEW HOME

My stay in the county jail awaiting transfer to prison was quick. I was almost immediately shipped off to the Northern California prison reception center. I intended to be Lil Andrew and not meet new people or talk to anyone. I just needed to find peace in my mind and calm myself down. I needed to stay out of trouble.

There is one thing that quickly became apparent to me. See, in prison you have nothing but your own thoughts and time. I spent many days in reflection. I set goals, which was something I had never done before. Well, let me clarify, I've never set positive goals. See, I had goals when I was selling drugs to amount a fortune. Now it was time to set goals to make me whole again.

Things were actually working out. I studied and took my GED. It gave me a feeling of accomplishment I had not known. When I delved down into my studies, I didn't have time to think about prison or the confinements it places on you. I then started taking correspondence courses for college. My mind was set on the sky as the limit. I got a job in the kitchen at that time. It was menial work but allowed me to sort of eat what I wanted. I told myself that I would never again in life let anyone other than me influence me.

Then a series of tragic events occurred that challenged me. First, my grandfather died. It bothered me to not be able to attend the funeral. Then my grandma died. She was my heart and that hurt me to my core. Then my dad was murdered. I felt hopelessness, as I couldn't do anything. As I sat within prison walls all that mattered to me was leaving this world, without me saying good-bye. I never had the chance to say I love you to my dad.

The evening I learned of my father's death, I imagined I was at his funeral. These words came from my mouth:

"My daddy was my everything. He was put here by God from the heavens above. My dad created me with the help of my beautiful, elegant, and spiritually gifted mother. Together they were married for 38 years. I tip my hat in admiration for the long commitment they shared. I am at awe and reflect on how much he cared for me and loved me.

For the 33 years, I have been on this earth, he made it a point to let the world know who his only son was. At times he believed in me more than I believed in myself. He represented me to others so much that, at times, I had to examine myself to check and see if he was accurate of the value he calculated me to be worth. And do you know what? Many times he was right. My daddy was my hype man. My Batman, to his Robin. Meaning whenever I needed direction, I would look towards my dad. He wasn't perfect in many ways, but I knew he loved and needed me as much as I needed him. He was my inspiration to rise to every occasion with the ingredients of perseverance, ambition, and fierceness. His favorite saying to me was, "We are Wadsworth!" At first, I used to brush it off as arrogance and pride, but now I recognize the significance of the

Wadsworth family. My family is just as important as any other family that is historically legendary. My late grandmother would tell you that.

As I close this message to my dad, that comes from my heart, I would like to add that I am painfully hurt, emotionally crushed, confused mentally, and physically drained. But through it all, it's up to me to become all I can be. We must leave this world one day, but it's up to us to leave a legacy. Daddy will forever be missed but never forgotten.

Those are the words that I would have said had I been given the freedom to attend my father's funeral.

✖ ✖ ✖

I placed myself into this world of prison madness. I will work on myself to rid myself of any reasons not to be present for future memories with my family that's still alive. See, for many years, I was an atheist. I felt there couldn't be a God with all the wrong and death that occurred in the world. But in 2013, I found God or should I say that he was always with me, I had just buried him deep inside me.

For the first time, I felt sorrow and regret about what happened to Antonio. I started to learn how to accept and take responsibility for my actions. I began to realize that violence is never the answer and that no one should lose his life to violence. I began to gain empathy for Antonio's family and what I took from them. I pondered the idea of the shooting happening the other way around. My family would have been devastated. I realized that there was a "domino effect" to my actions. That it not only affected me, but my family, and the community of Oakland also.

Now I'm in my mid 30's, and all that is on my mind is that Antonio's family can find healing. I've written letters to them which may never have been read. I write the letters to say that I'm genuinely sorry and to show his family that I, and I alone, am responsible for taking their son away.

I used to dream about having a magic wand. This wand would enable me to go back in time and erase all my wrongs. But then I would awaken and realize it was impossible.

As an adult, I do my best to teach the youngsters coming into the prison system that there is a better way. I know they are traveling the road that I have been down. I feel compelled to offer assistance. I need them to know there is a better way. I know that I have destroyed a family forever and by helping these kids, I can hope to save one. This is my obligation for repentance.

I know that I was only 16 years old at the time I committed my crime. But my ignorance and age will never be an excuse. There will never be a justifiable reason for why I held taking Antonio's life as an acceptable action. I can only hope and pray that his mom, dad, and grandparents find peace and his baby's mother and daughter can find solace and forgive me for taking him away. I know the pain that I have caused them is unforgivable.

I pray that my story can save the lives of some of the youth that read it. The game or street life will never, nor can it ever be justified. You're not alone, the feeling of abandonment will only go away if you learn to talk about it.

When I reflect on my life and past experiences up until now, I am humbled that I am blessed to have had the opportunity to share with you my regret, condolence, and sorrow. I will atone by sharing with you my shattered life now filled with new hopes and dreams. I can only hope that my thoughts don't offend anyone. They are thoughts of an adolescent that has matured and transformed his life. I especially hope I don't offend Antonio Young's family. I am deeply, and sincerely sorry for the pain I caused Antonio, his family, my family, along with the Oakland community. For my actions caused damage that cannot be repaired.

My wishes and prayers are that I can help transform the youth that may be heading down some of the paths that I traveled. I'm here to show that there are better ways and directions, rather than participating in the horrible and painful life of crime. Crime destroys lives and perpetuates agony, turmoil, and heartache. I have changed my life for the better, in many ways, with the hope of breaking the cycle of violence.

Again my book is not a glorification of the game; rather, it's intended to help, heal, and even bring peace. Also, I want to send my sincere apologies to the Young family. I'm only trying to express to the youth the truths of being misled in life and shine the light on all of my previous false beliefs. I'm not perfect, but I'm doing my best to play my part in the healing process and actively participate in the restoring and rebuilding our broken communities.

Sometimes prison can be a blessing. Since I have been incarcerated, I have lost some dear associates to the senseless violence in Brookfield. To name a few that was around me consistently was Lil Chris, Lil Vic, and Lil Jimmy. The ones that I hope can make a difference that are still there are Big Vee, Ken, Zody, DB (who has a book called Emotional Intelligence), and Fat Moe. If these people actually do as I plan on doing, Brookfield and East Oakland will be a very different place to live. To people like Damian Lillard that plays for the Portland Trailblazers, I tip my hat for working to rebuild the community of Oakland.

ANDREW'S PROCESS

It took a very long time for me to consider the need for change in my life. I recall my first thought process regarding change occurred while housed in juvenile hall. I was in reflection on the vile act that I had committed, which is the crime of murder. I looked back at my life and what it had turned into, a life prison sentence. I took into account when I first considered crime as okay. These thoughts occurred during the shuffle back and forth to court. I was still under the impression that I was the victim of the situation. My victim status was fueled by my own self-denial and unaccountability. Of course, it had to be everyone else's fault for what had occurred. These thoughts manifested when I was convicted at trial. I further echoed these thoughts to my appeal attorney in 2013. When my appeal was denied, it left me feeling trapped. I would not be released to continue on the destructive path I was on.

Parole denial left me with nothing but my own thoughts to ponder through. It was a moment that I needed most in life. I was forced to deal with the truth of my life and situation. I was the author of my circumstances and no one was to blame except for the man looking back at me, the man in the mirror. It was a dark moment as I replayed with new eyes what actually occurred that tragic day. I saw how terrible my actions were.

During this period, I was housed at High Desert State Prison, a maximum-security level 4 prison. This prison was full of politics and plagued with racial violence. It left other prisoners and me on lockdown status, confined to our cells many months out of the year. There was a real feeling of being trapped. I picked up a Bible and began to read it. The comfort of the stories in the Bible gave me insight into my own life. I prayed and asked God to enter my heart. It was as if my prayers had been answered as Senate Bill 260 ("The Second Chance Bill") was passed. It gave me hope at regaining a new life. My security points dropped and I was scheduled to transfer to old Folsom State Prison.

I knew that if I genuinely wanted change in my life, I had to change me. I had to change the way I thought about crime and those around me. Yet I had no life skills or coping mechanisms. These skills were critical as rage was still prevalent inside of me. I continued to read my Bible and ask God for strength.

When I was finally transferred to Old Folsom, I found an Insight class. It was a 6-month class that met for a few hours one day a week. Insight taught me reflective skills, how to look back at life to look forward. I saw what the causative factors that mislead me into street life were. I learned that aspects of my childhood were burdens I carried around. It taught me how scars from neglect and abandonment still echoed in my mind and heart. It was my first real perception into the ever-present sense of loneliness I knew.

My self-inquiries enabled me to grasp why, while in the streets, I sought relief in those like me. Basically, the people I placed in my life as role models had no real outlook or ambitions in life either. They accepted me because I, in fact, was one of them. The false sense of love I got was a mirror of their pain also. All of the fake hugs and the way they listened to me was a false sense of acknowledgment, yet it was consistent and made me feel a part of something bigger than myself. It was a false sense of family.

I was fortunate to be placed in a cell with a person that had real insights into life. This insightful gentleman was named Bey. He analyzed my crime and me and told me what was needed: "the truth." Bey said that when I recounted my story, I was still minimizing my role in the crime. He saw how I still felt that I was the real victim of the crime. Bey informed me that I had created a story to fit a perception and understanding I needed to give me justification for my action. I vividly remember one day I was telling Bey my story. He stopped me mid-sentence and said, "Tell your truth!" Initially, I replied. "I am telling the truth." He said, "Your truth," very strongly. I knew exactly what he meant and all I could do was shake my head towards the power of his statement. I could no longer try and justify my actions with this man. I had grown to have tremendous respect for him and learned that "my truth" wasn't "the truth." It was another light bulb moment for me that day: the realization that no matter how the reality of the horrible offense I committed may turn people against me, "my truth is my truth." All of the previous years of storytelling was just that, a lie and a story I made up to justify my actions. I knew if the real and authentic Andrew was to surface, I couldn't live a lie anymore and that I must tell "my truth" accurately. This is all thanks to Bey!

Once the Insight class ended, I took other life skill classes. I also began going to church regularly. This allowed me to start to feel a peace I had never known before. A correspondence (mail-based) college was available at this time. I enrolled in Coastline Community College and starting slowly with a few classes. I excelled by achieving high grades in the classes I took. It showed me that despite how I might have felt and been told, I am, in fact, smart.

✕ ✕ ✕

During this time a man named Michael Brown was murdered by a police officer. Michael Brown's murder by a police officer angered me but not in the same way it impacted some people. It didn't fill me with rage against the police but gave me insight into my crime. When I would see Brown's mother mourning and weeping on T.V., it reminded me of how Antonio's mom must feel and how I made her cry by tearing away her precious son. I was remorseful for the loss that I had created. It gave me a realistic visual of how my actions not only hurt Antonio but his family also.

After Brown's murder, there were several more police shootings of unarmed victims. To see Trevon Martin's mother and family going through the grieving process drove home how murder has a ripple effect on all people. This reality of how one death leaves a scar on all people again made me realize and sympathize for the Young family. Because up and until that point, I still had a lot of self-denial festering inside of me. But this defensive mechanism was flattened when I would see time and time again these mothers crying about their children's passing. Understanding more about the reality of the pain I caused the Young family and the Oakland community, made the change in my life more complete.

✕ ✕ ✕

I elected to transfer to San Quentin State Prison. When I arrived here at San Quentin, I learned the prison had over 50 programs available. This allowed me to further open my mind. I signed up to continue my education with Patten University Project.

The first group I signed up with is called "Project Choice." It gave me insight into how to transform myself into a responsible citizen; something I had never considered before. I also found employment with CAL-PIA Health in the Care Facility Maintenance (HFM) custodian program. This taught me the proper cleaning techniques utilized in the industrial world of cleaning hospitals. I went to work in the morning and attended college at night.

To participate in the HFM program, you have to agree to random drug testing. I had a bad week and smoked some weed. I was called in the next morning for a drug test. I tested positive for THC and was fired from the job. I didn't allow this set back to maim me. I enrolled in more programs with the free time I now had on my hands. I needed a better way to cope with life, so I enrolled in the programs called "T.R.U.S.T" and "Restorative Justice." These programs were different from anything I could have imagined. They brought in victims of crimes to speak to us. You can never imagine how impactful that was for me, to hear how crime had maimed their lives and their families. My empathy increased for "true" victims, which I no longer considered myself to be. I was actually the monster and culprit they talked about. Their testimonies reminded me of how I destroyed Antonio's family.

The Restorative Justice program, in particular, hit me like a ton of bricks. I feel such a program should be mandatory for all prisoners regardless of the commitment offense. This program helped me to be able to empathize with the actual crime victim. I always considered crimes like rape, murder, kidnapping, and torture to be unforgivable. But after attending the class for 3 years, I have a different outlook.

While in class, I was able to hear the stories shared by people who suffered from horrific types of crimes. To listen to their heartfelt testimonies humbled me. I learned that some of the victims have compassion for their perpetrators. That is still something that I find hard to understand to this day. However, I began to realize that for some victims to heal, they must first forgive the offender.

I remember watching one impactful documentary. It showed a crying mother, whose daughter was raped and then murdered by a man. In this documentary, she requested a sit down with the offender while he was in prison. She was granted her request and she told the man that she forgave him for his crime. They hugged each other at the end of the documentary. This was done without any rage or anger. This visualization made me cry and opened my heart to the real power of forgiveness. I learned the vital force that comes from this process. I realized that to forgive doesn't mean to forget, but that forgiveness means healing. This class taught me that healing doesn't remove scars, but it does stop the infection.

"Without forgiveness, we remain tethered to the person who harmed us. We are bound to the chains of bitterness, tied together, trapped. Until we can forgive the person who harmed us, that person will hold the keys to our happiness, that person will be our jailor. When we forgive, we take back control of our own fate and our feelings. We become our own liberator."

This excerpt was quoted in The Book of Healing and can be found in The Book of Joy, written by his Holiness the Dalai Lama, Archbishop Desmond Tutu, and Douglas Abrams. A compelling read that gave me a real insight into how some victims can forgive criminals for the most heinous of crimes.

I then enrolled in Criminal Gang Anonymous (CGA). This group taught me all about the criminal thinking I had formulated over the years and how those thoughts made me desensitize myself to the crimes I had committed and in general.

I also enrolled in Guiding Rage into Power (GRIP), which was a compelling group. This was my comprehension into the lack of mindfulness I held during the crimes I committed. I learned how to read body language and signals given off when people are faced with imminent danger. I learned that there are many stages to violence and pain origins and how these traumas become driving forces for crimes.

GRIP and its sponsors have become very special to me. Susan Shakur and Monique, GRIP facilitators, helped me during the time when I grieved from my father being murdered. They taught me how to "sit in the fire" while I felt all was lost. They taught me how to face and deal with all the emotions that came up, how to deal with the rage that filled me, and mostly how to heal. I could use emotional intelligence instead of acting out in violence. These new coping skills helped me to mature into the man I am today.

This recount of my transformation may seem as if it happened overnight, but truthfully it has taken years of self-reflection and intentional effort. The result being I have learned how to open up and share my mistakes without shame.

The biggest obstacle of my transformation rested on my belief system. I really had to learn the difference from what I considered was right and understand it as wrong. This caused many days filled with personal conflict because my old belief system would try to creep into my current mindset and cloud my judgment. This was the belief system that had destroyed the first half of my life.

I am now fully aware of what I did wrong and mostly how I got there. I have learned that my crime doesn't define me or my future. I no longer share or admire the disgraceful life of my past.

My history is there as a deterrent as to what not to ever consider doing again. I am a child of God, filled with integrity. I have so much empathy for those I have hurt. It brings tears to my eyes. I know my purpose is to give back to the world, to help aid in the youths' development and healing for those that need it and to contribute to restoring sanity to the neighborhoods I worked so hard to destroy. It pains my heart to realize that at 16 years of age, I had become the monster and villain that horror books are written about. I devalued life and thought of human beings as objects. I believed that violence was the way of the world. I am no longer that person. I will never make excuses for my actions again. It took a very long time to come out of denial and to finally accept responsibility for my actions. I, and I alone, am responsible and accountable for my crimes. My goal is to amend, either directly or indirectly with all those I have harmed. I vow to be an asset to the world instead of a burden.

Be positive and stay blessed!
Do good! Love your neighbor and self!

Tio MacDonald
East Oakland Times
Chief Editor

www.ingramcontent.com/pod-product-compliance
Lightning Source LLC
Chambersburg PA
CBHW071341290326
41933CB00040B/1972

www.ingramcontent.com/pod-product-compliance
Lightning Source LLC
Chambersburg PA
CBHW071347290326
41933CB00041B/3023